My Very Own

Poetry Collection

101 Poems for Kindergartners

by Betsy Franco

Teaching Resource Center

For Denise Dauler, a wonderful kindergarten teacher
who lets me visit her classroom every morning

Acknowledgments
"My Shadow" is based on a poem with the same title from *Poem of the Week, Book 1*, Teaching Resource Center, 1998.
"When I Feel Friendly" is based on the poem "Nice and Friendly" from *Poem of the Week, Book 1*, Teaching Resource Center, 1998.
"The Last Day of School" is based on the poem "Goodbye, Buddy" from *The Buddy Book*, Teaching Resource Center, 1997.
"A Star with Wings" is based on a poem with the same title from *Thematic Poems: Creepy Crawlies*, Scholastic, Inc., 2000.
"The Pink Pigs" is based on the poem "Pink-Skinned Pigs" from *Thematic Poems: On the Farm*, Scholastic, Inc., 2000
"I Like to Be Silly" is based on the poem "A Laugh, A Giggle" from *Pocket Poetry Mini-Books*, Scholastic, Inc., 2002.

Published by
14525 SW Millikan, #11910 Beaverton, OR 97005-2343
1-800-833-3389
www.trcabc.com

Design and production by Janis Poe
Illustrations by Linda Starr
Edited by Laura Woodard

Printed in the United States of America
ISBN: 1-56785-061-8

Table of Contents

Introduction

Poetry is such a perfect way to introduce kindergartners to the early stages of literacy. It's brief. It's fun. It's got rhythm!

The poems in this personal poetry collection have been carefully crafted to meet the specific needs of kindergartners. Themes and topics used by most kindergarten teachers are the focus of the collection. There are poems about friendship and family, the seasons, the first and last day of school, animals, and much, much more.

Most of the poems are from four to six lines long, making tracking easier for the emergent reader. The longer poems have very few words per line or include lots of repetition. In addition, an "anchor word" begins nearly every title and poem. Having a high frequency word as the first word of the title and the poem gives kinders a sense of confidence. Once they've read a word that is an old friend, off they go!

Reading a poem in many forms makes it fun for kinders to practice and develop their reading skills. For individual, group, and whole class work, we've provided the tools you need. Each poem has a student poem page with an engaging illustration. This enables children to create their own personal poetry collections. For group and center work, we've provided strips that fit into the Desktop Pocket Chart. We've also included instructions for enlarging the poems for use as poetry posters.

Versatility

There are enough poems in the collection to present at least two per week. You can use the poems in order or choose them according to the themes your class is studying. You can also focus on poems that enhance a particular math, social studies, or science lesson.

The math poems are "Happy Birthday to Me," "The Estimation Jar," "The 100th Day of School," "Off to the Moon," "The Shapes," "The Numbers," and "100."

Social studies topics are sprinkled throughout the collection under the themes *All About You and Me; Family and Friends; At School; Around Town; Transportation; My Country, My Earth, My World;* and *Holidays.*

The science poems include "We Recycle" and all the poems under the themes *Seasons and Weather, Bugs,* and *All About Animals.*

What You've Got

- At least two poems for every week of the year
- Sets of poems that match your kindergarten themes
- Suggestions in this introduction for using the poems to teach high frequency words and emergent reading skills
- Suggestions in this introduction for making the poems personal and interactive and for using them as creative springboards
- Poetry strips and an illustration that fit into the Desktop Pocket Chart

Useful Accessories

The following accessories can be useful when extending the poems:

Desktop Pocket Chart
My Very Own Poetry Collection includes strips for each poem that fit into the 12" x 16" Desktop Pocket Chart. You can use the poems for intimate group work with the help of this miniature pocket chart.

Wikki Stix
Made of waxed yarn, Wikki Stix stick to almost any surface, including the student poem and the Desktop Pocket Chart. They are perfect for underlining or circling words in the poem with the featured phonics element.

Highlighting Tape
This removable, colorful, transparent tape can be used to highlight key words or phrases on the Desktop Pocket Chart.

Sticky Notes
Sticky notes are useful for making poems interactive. You can use them to rewrite words on the Desktop Pocket Chart.

Standard Pocket Chart and Sentence Strips
If you choose to, you can reproduce the poems on standard pocket chart strips for whole-class or group instruction.

How the Book Is Organized

Student Poems

For every week of the year, you have at least two poems, in large print for easy reading. You can make a copy of the poem for each child. Each child can have his or her own personal poetry collection.

Strips for the Desktop Pocket Chart

You've got all the tools you need for group work. Copy the enlarged strips (starting on page 115) onto index tag, cut them apart, and display them in the Desktop Pocket Chart. That way, you'll have a poem for many eyes to see. Groups of children can interact with the poem using this intimate, yet practical medium.

Poetry Posters

You can enlarge the poems to poster size (11" by 14" @130%) using a copier that allows for this. You may want to ask for assistance at your local copy center.

Suggestions for Going Further

The introduction (pp. 3–13) provides an extensive array of activities that will help you get the most from the poetry. The suggestions show how you can use the poems to focus on high frequency words, consonants, and other phonetic elements; rhyming words; repetitive phrases; and other treasures buried in the poems. The suggestions also include ideas for making the poems personal and interactive for the children and for tapping children's own poetic talents.

How to Use the Elements of the Book

There are many ways to use the personal poetry collection with your students.

Ways to Use the Student Poems

- Photocopy the poem for each child.
- Enjoy the poem for the beauty of the words, the rhythm, and the content.
- Add blanks to the poem by covering certain words so that children can interact with it and personalize it.
- Use the poem to point out high frequency words, beginning consonants, phonograms, and/or short and long vowel sounds.
- Have each child create a personal poetry collection with a decorated cover.
- Enlarge the poem to 11" by 14" and use it as a poem poster in the classroom.
- When the collection is complete, send it home to be read with family members.

Suggestions for Going Further with the Student Poems

Talk about the title. In short poems, the title can be a very important part of the poem. Let children predict what the poem will be about.

Have children circle or underline the words in the poem that begin with the consonant you are studying.

Invite children to underline the repetitive words or phrases in the poem.

Work together to find the rhyming words and underline them. Emphasize them as you're reading the poem aloud.

Talk about the humor in the poem or the twist at the end.

Have fun guessing the answers to the riddles about a red rubber ball, a bear, and a whale.

54   Transportation

All Kinds of Transportation

A bus,
a train,
a boat,
a plane,
some trucks and cars
out on the street,
a taxicab,
and my two feet!

©2002 Teaching Resource Center

Clap to the rhythm of the poem.

Have individuals, partners, or groups recite the poem to develop oral literacy. Or memorize the poem and recite it together.

Have children read the poem with an older buddy, taking turns reading every other line.

The Fall Leaves

The wind blew. Yahoo!
The leaves are falling
on my head,
brown,
yellow,
orange,
and red.

Invite children to make a border for the poem or an additional illustration.

The Sounds at School

Grrr, grrr.
The sharpener.
Vroom, vroom.
The lawnmower.
Brrrring, Brrrring.
The last bell rings.

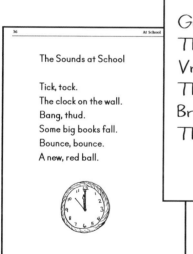

36   At School

The Sounds at School

Tick, tock.
The clock on the wall.
Bang, thud.
Some big books fall.
Bounce, bounce.
A new, red ball.

©2002 Teaching Resource Center

Help children write a new verse. New verses don't have to rhyme.

Down On The Farm   103

The Silly Farm

The sheep said oink.
The duck said moo.
The farmer said cock-a-doodle-doo.
The cows just didn't know what to do.

Moo

©2002 Teaching Resource Center

The Silly Farm

The horse said quack.
The goat said neigh.
The cows said cock-a-doodle-doo.
The farmer didn't know what to do.

As a class, write a new poem using the original as a model.

Let childen write a con-
crete poem that is inside a
special shape. Children
can use the Valentine
poem as a model.

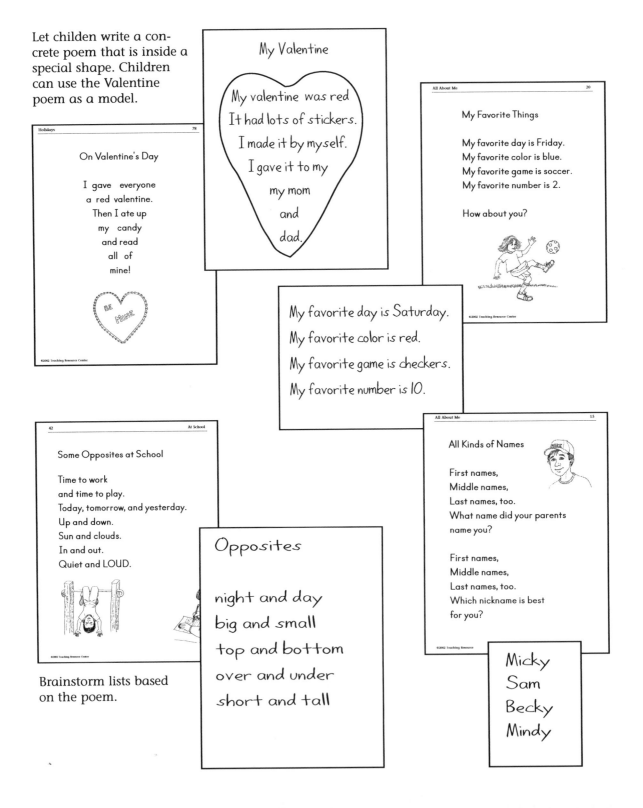

My Valentine

My valentine was red
It had lots of stickers.
I made it by myself.
I gave it to my
my mom
and
dad.

Holidays   78

On Valentine's Day

I gave everyone
a red valentine.
Then I ate up
my candy
and read
all of
mine!

BE
MINE

©2002 Teaching Resource Center

All About Me   20

My Favorite Things

My favorite day is Friday.
My favorite color is blue.
My favorite game is soccer.
My favorite number is 2.

How about you?

©2002 Teaching Resource Center

My favorite day is Saturday.
My favorite color is red.
My favorite game is checkers.
My favorite number is 10.

42   At School

Some Opposites at School

Time to work
and time to play.
Today, tomorrow, and yesterday.
Up and down.
Sun and clouds.
In and out.
Quiet and LOUD.

©2002 Teaching Resource Center

Brainstorm lists based
on the poem.

Opposites

night and day
big and small
top and bottom
over and under
short and tall

All About Me   15

All Kinds of Names

First names,
Middle names,
Last names, too.
What name did your parents
name you?

First names,
Middle names,
Last names, too.
Which nickname is best
for you?

©2002 Teaching Resource

Micky
Sam
Becky
Mindy

My Feelings

My feelings go up.
My feelings go down.
Sometimes I am happy.
Sometimes I frown.
But most of the time,
I feel just fine!

Make a web based on the poem.

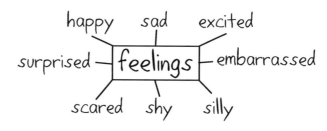

happy   sad   excited
surprised — feelings — embarrassed
scared   shy   silly

Act out the poem.

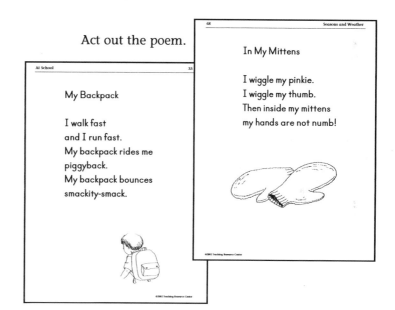

My Backpack

I walk fast
and I run fast.
My backpack rides me
piggyback.
My backpack bounces
smackity-smack.

In My Mittens

I wiggle my pinkie.
I wiggle my thumb.
Then inside my mittens
my hands are not numb!

Our Growing Family

We used to have four.
But my family just grew.
Now we have five.
The baby is new!

Make a graph based on the poem.

How Many in Our Families					
		X	X		
		X	X		
	X	X	X		
	X	X	X	X	
X	X	X	X	X	X
2	3	4	5	6	7

Happy Birthday to Me

My birthday!
My birthday!
I stand up and cheer!
My next birthday party
will be in a year!

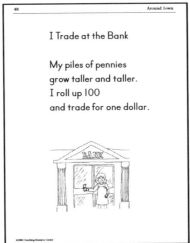

I Trade at the Bank

My piles of pennies
grow taller and taller.
I roll up 100
and trade for one dollar.

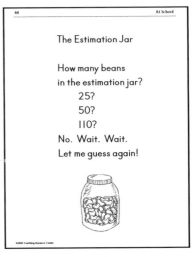

The Estimation Jar

How many beans
in the estimation jar?
25?
50?
110?
No. Wait. Wait.
Let me guess again!

Explore the math in the poem. After reading "Happy Birthday to Me," figure out how many times a year a birthday comes. Explore how many months or days there are between birthdays.

Use manipulatives to act out the math poems. Stack up pennies in groups of ten and count them.

After reading "The Estimation Jar," have children guess how many beans there are in the class's own estimation jar.

Ways to Use the Desktop Pocket Chart

- Copy the poem strips and the illustration from the student poem page onto index tag.
- Cut out the strips and the illustration.
- Reconstruct the poem in the Desktop Pocket Chart. We've numbered each line to minimize confusion. You can keep the numbers or cut them off.
- Gather a group of children. Read the poem once or twice for them. Track the words as you go, using a pointer or your finger. Or frame the word you are reading with a framer or your palms.
- Have children recite the poem with you, again tracking each word. You may find it helpful to add and read one strip at a time.
- Work with the poem for a week. Read it together about ten times in all.
- Place the poem in a center and have children work in pairs. They can read the poem by pointing at each word, highlight words they know, and put mixed-up pocket chart strips back in order.

Suggestions for Going Further with the Desktop Pocket Chart

The Rain

<u>Out</u> <u>on</u> <u>the</u> farm

<u>and</u> <u>all</u> <u>over</u> town,

<u>it</u> never rains <u>up</u>.

<u>It</u> always rains <u>down</u>.

Use nonpermanent markers, Wikki Stix, or highlighting tape to highlight the high frequency words in the poem. They are old friends. Practice the unfamiliar words before reading the poem together.

<u>What</u> the Sheep <u>Wear</u>

In <u>winter</u>, their <u>wool</u>

is <u>warm</u> and full.

In spring, they don't <u>wear</u>

anything.

Let children highlight the words in the poem that begin with the consonant you are studying.

My Shadow

When I swing a <u>bat</u>,

When I wear a <u>hat</u>,

When I <u>pat</u> a <u>cat</u>,

My shadow does <u>that</u>!

Invite children to highlight words in the poem that have the phonogram or the short or long vowel sound you are studying.

I Love <u>Hot Fudge</u>

But <u>hot fudge</u> on meat balls,

<u>Hot fudge</u> on rice,

<u>Hot fudge</u> on noodles

is not very nice.

A <u>Lot</u> of Pancakes

They flip

They <u>flop</u>.

I put butter on <u>top</u>.

And when they are <u>hot</u>,

I eat a whole <u>lot</u>!

What <u>Trucks</u> Do

<u>Trucks</u> dig.

<u>Trucks</u> crunch.

<u>Trucks</u> munch recycling

for their lunch.

Encourage children to discover the repetitive words or phrases in the poem. Highlight them.

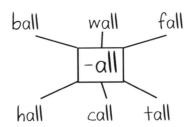

Have children find the rhyming words and highlight them. Emphasize them as you're reading the poem aloud.

Make lists or webs of rhyming words on chart paper. Use words from the poem and add new ones, too.

Have fun reading the poem in two voices. Explain, "It's my turn then your turn."

Use sticky notes to cover words in the poem. Let children suggest new words to write in their places to personalize or change the poem. Alternatively, you can use blank word cards made from heavy paper to cover and replace words. (Cards should be about 2" long by 1" high.)

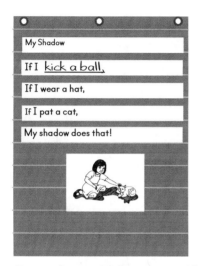

My Shadow

If I _kick a ball,_

If I wear a hat,

If I pat a cat,

My shadow does that!

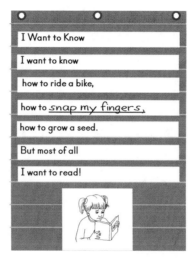

I Want to Know

I want to know

how to ride a bike,

how to _snap my fingers,_

how to grow a seed.

But most of all

I want to read!

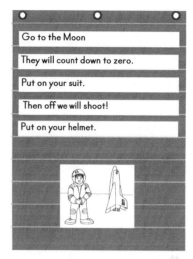

Go to the Moon

They will count down to zero.

Put on your suit.

Then off we will shoot!

Put on your helmet.

Cover phrases in the poem with blank strips and let children interact with the poem by rewriting the phrases. Strips should be about 1" high. The new lines don't have to rhyme.

Mix up the strips of the poem and have children rearrange them. Note that this is a fun activity for a center.

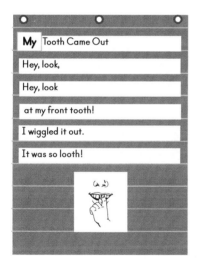

My Tooth Came Out

Hey, look,

Hey, look

at my front tooth!

I wiggled it out.

It was so looth!

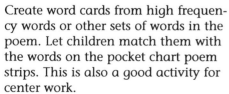

Create word cards from high frequency words or other sets of words in the poem. Let children match them with the words on the pocket chart poem strips. This is also a good activity for center work.

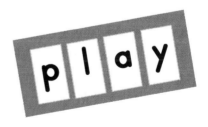

Have children use letters to build a high frequency word or another word from the poem.

We Are Special

You can look on the land.
You can look on the sea.
There is no one exactly
like you or like me.

All Kinds of Names

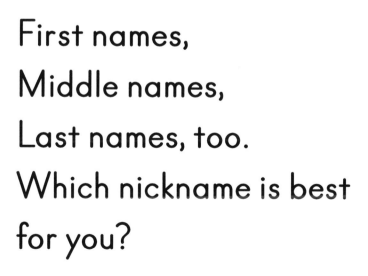

First names,
Middle names,
Last names, too.
What name did your parents
name you?

First names,
Middle names,
Last names, too.
Which nickname is best
for you?

My Feelings

My feelings go up.
My feelings go down.
Sometimes I am happy.
Sometimes I frown.
But most of the time,
I feel just fine!

I Want to Know

I want to know
how to ride a bike,
how to jump a rope,
how to grow a seed.
But most of all
I want to read!

The First Time

I can tie my shoe
really tight!
Come check it out.
I did it right!

Happy Birthday to Me

My birthday!
My birthday!
I stand up and cheer!
My next birthday party
will be in a year!

My Favorite Things

My favorite day is Friday.
My favorite color is blue.
My favorite game is soccer.
My favorite number is 2.

How about you?

My Tooth Came Out

Hey, look,
Hey, look
at my front tooth!
I wiggled it out.
It was so looth!

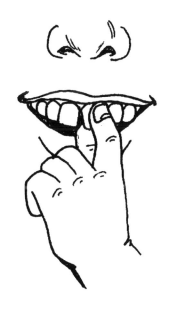

I Love Hot Fudge

But hot fudge on meat balls,
Hot fudge on rice,
Hot fudge on noodles
is not very nice.

A Lot of Pancakes

They flip.
They flop.
I put butter on top.
And when they are hot,
I eat a whole lot!

My Pets

My mom says no croaking.
So we do not have a frog.
My mom says no barking.
So we do not have a dog.

But my mom said okay
to two fishes today!

My Cat Is Up a Tree

My cat goes up.
She will not come down.
My cat should stay
down on the ground.

My Shadow

When I swing a bat,
When I wear a hat,
When I pat a cat,
My shadow does that!

A Recipe for a Family

A family needs
a roof above.
Then mix in caring
and mix in love.

Our Growing Family

We used to have four.

But my family just grew.

Now we have five.

The baby is new!

My Grandma

I know Grandma loves me
when she gives me a hug.
I feel warm.
I feel happy.
I feel very, very snug.

When I Feel Friendly

I say hi to Peg.
Peg says hi to Meg.
Meg says hi to Ron.
Ron says hi to John.
When I am feeling friendly,
I like to pass it on.

Friends

Friends help when you are sad.

Friends listen when you are mad.

Friends laugh.

Friends play.

Friends make you feel okay.

I Make a New Friend

What is your name?
Do you want to play?
We can be friends
starting today!

My First Day of School

My mom came with me.
My dad came with me,
for my very first day.
Yippee!
Yippee!

When I Walk to School

I hop.

I skip.

I eat a snack.

I kick a rock

and jump over a crack!

My Backpack

I walk fast
and I run fast.
My backpack rides me
piggyback.
My backpack bounces
smackity-smack.

The Sounds at School

Tick, tock.

The clock on the wall.

Bang, thud.

Some big books fall.

Bounce, bounce.

A new, red ball.

Our School Garden

We cannot grow popcorn
or jellybeans.
But we can grow pumpkins
for Halloween!

Get Ready!

Clean up all the blocks.
Sit down in your seat.
Shhh. Shhh. Be quiet.
The teacher has a treat!

For Hot Lunch

Hot ribs

Hot dogs

Hot pizza pie

Hot burgers

Hot tacos

Hot French fries

I Lost My Coat

At home,
At school,
I looked all around.
Hey, here is my coat
in the Lost and Found!

Look-Alike Day

We are copycats
on Look-Alike Day.
We call our friends
and dress the same way.

Some Opposites at School

Time to work

and time to play.

Today, tomorrow, and yesterday.

Up and down.

Sun and clouds.

In and out.

Quiet and LOUD.

When I Shared My Cat

When I shared my cat,
he was scared about that.
He tried to eat
our parakeet.
He ran around fast.
But we got him at last!

The Estimation Jar

How many beans
in the estimation jar?
25?
50?
110?
No. Wait. Wait.
Let me guess again!

Who Am I?

You throw me.

You catch me.

You bounce me on the wall. (Ouch!)

You dribble.

You kick me.

I am a red rubber _____!

The Last Day of School

Good-bye, my school friends.
We really had a ball.
I will see you in the summer
or back at school
next fall.

At the Library

Every day
at the librar-y,
every book
you see
is free!

I Trade at the Bank

My piles of pennies
grow taller and taller.
I roll up 100
and trade for one dollar.

At the Ice Cream Store

It is hard to pick
which one to lick
and which kind of cone
to munch and crunch.

The Police

I wave at the police car.
It is black and it is white.
The police keep me safe
all day and all night.

The Fire Fighters

Fire! Fire!
9 - 1 - 1
The firefighters stay
till the work is done.

What the Mailman Had

A letter for mom.
A letter for dad.
That is what the mailman had.

One more thing!
A box for me!
A birthday gift!
What could it be?

Some Animal Transportation

The little frog has legs to hop.

The monkey swings from tree to tree.

The green snake wiggles.

The birds all fly.

The penguin swims in the cold cold sea.

All Kinds of Transportation

A bus,
a train,
a boat,
a plane,
some trucks and cars
out on the street,
a taxicab,
and my two feet!

What Trucks Do

Trucks dig.
Trucks crunch.
Trucks munch recycling
for their lunch.

When You Ride a Bike

Stop at every
stop sign.
Show turns
with your hand.

Always wear
your helmet.
It can save you
when you land.

The Train

I show my ticket.
Then clackity-clack,
clackity-clack,
clackity-clack.
The train goes speeding
down the track.

What is Fast, Faster, Fastest?

My skateboard is fast.
My scooter is faster.
But when I am late,
my bike is just great!

The Plane Ride

My seat belt goes click.
Up, up we go.
Then out my window,
clouds put on a show!

Go to the Moon

Put on your helmet.
Put on your suit.
They will count down to zero.
Then off we will shoot!

10, 9, 8, 7, 6, 5, 4, 3, 2, 1, 0
Blastoff!

Our Flag

Our flag! Our flag!
You are red, white, and blue.
We stand and we say
the pledge to you.

We Recycle

We recycle each paper.
We recycle each can.
We help save the earth.
That is our plan!

All Over the World

All over the world, kids
    run and jump,
    play with friends,
    hug their parents,
    go to school.
Just like me!
That is cool!

In All Kinds of Weather

A warm rain.

A lot of snow.

A sunny sky.

A big rainbow.

In all kinds of weather,

we still play together.

The Fall Leaves

The wind blew. Yahoo!
The leaves are falling
on my head,
brown,
yellow,
orange,
and red.

The Apples in Fall

Yellow, red, or green.
Shiny, hard, and clean.

Sour or sweet.
Crunchy to eat!

Snow

Snowflakes
Snowfall
Snowman
Snowball

Snowball fight
one and all!

In My Mittens

I wiggle my pinkie.
I wiggle my thumb.
Then inside my mittens
my hands are not numb!

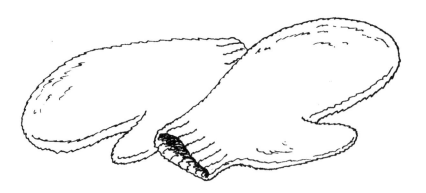

When It Snows

It is very quiet
when it snows.
The snowflakes softly
tap my nose.

The Spring Things

The days are warm.
The baby birds
flap flap
their baby wings.
The flowers grow.
The winds blow.
It must be spring!

In the Wind

In windy weather
grab your hat.
But let your kite
go way up high,
red and yellow
in the clear, blue sky.

In Summer

On a hot summer day,
we try to stay
as cool and wet
as we can get.

All Year Round

In fall we walk on yellow leaves.

In winter we walk on ice and snow.

In spring we walk on flower beds.

In summer we walk on grass and then,

in fall, we start all over again.

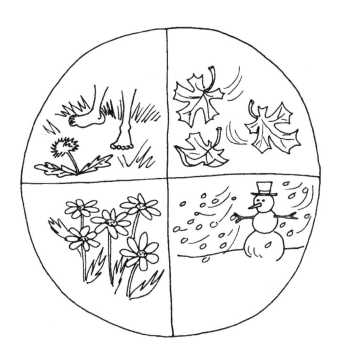

On Halloween

A black hat.
A small hat.
A funny hat.
A tall hat.

What will I be on Halloween?
A bat?
A pumpkin?
A clown?
A queen?

On Thanksgiving

Thank you for my family.
Thank you for my friends.
Thank you for the big blue sky.
Thanks for turkey and pumpkin pie.

For Dr. Martin Luther King, Jr.

For Dr. Martin Luther King,
freedom

peace

friends

and love

were all of the important things.

The 100th Day of School

We are counting the days
in lots of ways.
After 99,
comes the 100th day!

On Valentine's Day

I gave   everyone
a red valentine.
Then I ate up
my   candy
and read
all of
mine!

On St. Patrick's Day

It is hard to catch
a leprechaun.
You think you have him.
But then he is gone!

The Days of the Week

Count them up.
Seven days.

Five for school.
Two for play.

Monday
Tuesday
Wednesday
Thursday
Friday
Saturday
and Sunday.

The Colors

The sun is yellow.
Apples are red.
The sky and the sea are blue.

The grass is green.
Owls are brown.
The night is black. Whooo.
Whooooo.

The Shapes

The playground has
rectangles,
circles,
and squares.
But there are no
triangles
anywhere.

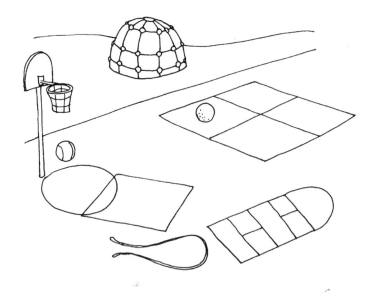

The Numbers

The numbers like to
stay in line.
1, 2, 3, 4, 5, 6, 7, 8, 9.
The numbers like to
do their tricks,
like 3 plus 3 always makes 6!

Some Bug Colors

What is green? a grasshopper
What is red? ants on a tree
What is orange? a butterfly
What is black? this spider on me!

The Spider in the Car

Hey, little spider
living in our car.
Your spider web tells me
where you are.

I wish you would decide
to go and live outside.

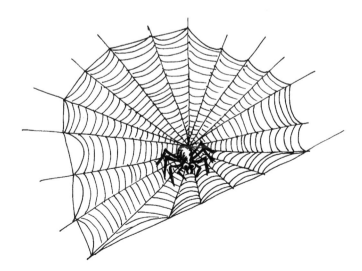

A Yucky Bug

I have seen an ant.

I have seen a bee.

I have seen a fly.

I have seen a flea.

But this little bug

is the yuckiest bug

that I will ever ever see.

Our Class Has Silkworms

Our silkworms get fat.
They eat lots of leaves.
Then they make the cocoons
that they know how to weave.

Inside they grow wings
that they show in the spring.

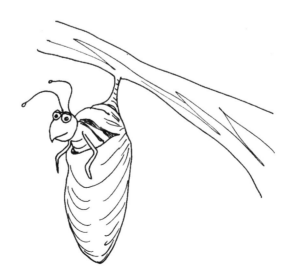

The Bees

Bees are fuzzy.
Bees are buzzy.
But stay far away.
Bees do not like to play.

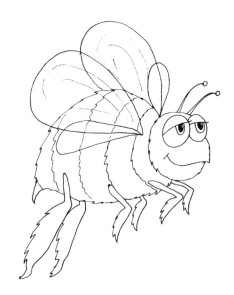

A Star With Wings

Sometimes it seems
like a little star
has fallen
from the sky.
But when I see
the star has wings,
I know it is a firefly.

The Boy Ladybugs

Do the boy ladybugs
hear their name
and say *ugh*?

Some Animal Names

The woodpecker pecks.
The grasshopper hops.
The stingray stings.
I wish it would stop.

Some Baby Animals

A kitten is a baby cat.

A colt is a baby horse.

A calf can be a baby whale,

or a baby cow, of course.

A Lot of Eggs

Here is a blue egg.
Who is inside?
A baby robin.
What a surprise!

Here is a small egg.
Who is inside?
A baby fish.
What a surprise!

Here is a long egg.
Who is inside?
A baby snake.
What a surprise!

Here is an egg
in super-size.
A dinosaur!
What a surprise!

The Turtle

We helped out the turtle
who was crossing the street,
so he would not get squashed
by cars or by feet.

When Alligators Grow

Everybody seems to love
a baby alligator.
But when she is big and scary,
everybody seems to hate her.

The Great White Shark

The great white shark
does not go to sleep.
Does he ever get tired
of swimming in the deep?

If I Were an Octopus

I would call a friend.

I would drum a beat.

I would play a game.

I would eat a treat.

I would jump a rope.

I would watch TV.

All at the very same time, you see!

A Penguin

Slip, slide,
she glides on her tummy.
Jump, dive,
she eats something yummy.

Who Is It?

This mammal has
a whale of a tail.
Watch out!
It spouts water
all about!

I Sleep in a Cave

I go very deep
in a cave to sleep
until birds in spring
begin to cheep.
Who am I?

All About Bats

At night,
the bats all fly around.
In the day,
the bats sleep upside down!

Some Animal Homes

Crabs live in sand.

Snails live on leaves.

Birds live in trees.

Whales live in seas.

My cat is the home

for lots and lots of fleas.

The Silly Farm

The sheep said oink.

The duck said moo.

The farmer said cock-a-doodle-doo.

The cows just didn't know what to do.

In the Morning

Go milk the cow.

Look under the hens.

Then hold your nose!

Feed the pigs in their pens.

What the Sheep Wear

In winter, their wool
is warm and full.
In spring, they don't wear
anything.

The Pink Pigs

The fat, pink pigs
roll in the mud
because it is no fun
to get a piggy sunburn
in the hot, summer sun.

100

I would not like to have
100 brothers or
or 100 little sisters.
But I would like to have
100 dogs or
100 cats with whiskers.

What Can You Pop?

Pop a drink box.
Pop a sack.
Pop your bubble gum.
Yum! Yum! Yum!

Pop a trash bag.
Pop some popcorn
Pop the bubble wrap.
Snap! Snap! Snap!

Please Tickle Me

Tickle me one.

Tickle me two.

Tickle me under my sock and shoe.

Tickle me three.

Tickle me four.

Tickle until I scream, "No more!"

Some Somersault Fun

Come and join us.
Have some fun.
Do some somersaults in the sun.

We do somersaults
in the park.
We only stop when it gets dark.

It Fits

An egg fits well
inside its shell.

A banana must feel
snug in its peel.

And my skin hides
all my insides!

The Rain

Out on the farm
and all over town,
it never rains up.
It always rains down.

I Like to Be Silly

It starts with a smile
that shows on my face.
But soon I am laughing
all over the place.

How Do You Do, Glue?

How do you do, glue?

Take a look, book.

Never again, pen.

See you later, calculator!

We Are Special

2 You can look on the land.

3 You can look on the sea.

4 There is no one exactly

5 like you or like me.

All Kinds of Names

2 First names,

3 Middle names,

4 Last names, too.

5 What name did your parents

6 name you?

7 First names,

8 Middle names,

9 Last names, too.

10 Which nickname is best

11 for you?

1. My Feelings

2. My feelings go up.

3. My feelings go down.

4. Sometimes I am happy.

5. Sometimes I frown.

6. But most of the time,

7. I feel just fine!

1. I Want to Know

2 I want to know

3 how to ride a bike,

4 how to jump a rope,

5 how to grow a seed.

6 But most of all

7 I want to read!

1 The First Time

2 I can tie my shoe

3 really tight!

4 Come check it out.

5 I did it right!

1 Happy Birthday to Me

2 My birthday!

3 My birthday!

4 I stand up and cheer!

5 My next birthday party

6 will be in a year!

1 My Favorite Things

2 My favorite day is Friday.

3 My favorite color is blue.

4 My favorite game is soccer.

5 My favorite number is 2.

6 How about you?

1 My Tooth Came Out

2 Hey, look,

3 Hey, look

4 at my front tooth!

5 I wiggled it out.

6 It was so looth!

1 I Love Hot Fudge

2 But hot fudge on meat balls,

3 Hot fudge on rice,

4 Hot fudge on noodles

5 is not very nice.

A Lot of Pancakes

1 A Lot of Pancakes

2 They flip.

3 They flop.

4 I put butter on top.

5 And when they are hot,

6 I eat a whole lot!

1 My Pets

2 My mom says no croaking.

3 So we do not have a frog.

4 My mom says no barking.

5 So we do not have a dog.

6 But my mom said okay

7 to two fishes today!

1 My Cat Is Up a Tree

2 My cat goes up.

3 She will not come down.

4 My cat should stay

5 down on the ground.

1 My Shadow

2 When I swing a bat,

3 When I wear a hat,

4 When I pat a cat,

5 My shadow does that!

1 A Recipe for a Family

2 A family needs

3 a roof above.

4 Then mix in caring

5 and mix in love.

1 Our Growing Family

2 We used to have four.

13 But my family just grew.

4 Now we have five.

5 The baby is new!

1 My Grandma

2 I know Grandma loves me

3 when she gives me a hug.

4 I feel warm.

5 I feel happy.

6 I feel very, very snug.

1 When I Feel Friendly

2 I say hi to Peg.

3 Peg says hi to Meg.

4 Meg says hi to Ron.

5 Ron says hi to John.

6 When I am feeling friendly,

7 I like to pass it on.

1 Friends

2 Friends help when you are sad.

3 Friends listen when you are mad.

4 Friends laugh.

5 Friends play.

6 Friends make you feel okay.

1 I Make a New Friend

2 What is your name?

3 Do you want to play?

4 We can be friends

5 starting today!

1 My First Day of School

2 My mom came with me.

3 My dad came with me,

4 for my very first day.

5 Yippee!

16 Yippee!

When I Walk to School

2 I hop.

3 I skip.

4 I eat a snack.

5 I kick a rock

6 and jump over a crack!

My Backpack

2 I walk fast

3 and I run fast.

4 My backpack rides me

5 piggyback.

6 My backpack bounces

7 smackity-smack.

1 The Sounds at School

2 Tick, tock.

3 The clock on the wall.

4 Bang, thud.

5 Some big books fall.

6 Bounce, bounce.

7 A new, red ball.

1 Our School Garden

2 We cannot grow popcorn

3 or jellybeans.

4 But we can grow pumpkins

5 for Halloween!

1 Get Ready!

2 Clean up all the blocks.

3 Sit down in your seat.

4 Shhh. Shhh. Be quiet.

5 The teacher has a treat!

1 For Hot Lunch

2 Hot ribs

3 Hot dogs

4 Hot pizza pie

5 Hot burgers

6 Hot tacos

7 Hot French fries

1 I Lost My Coat

2 At home,

3 At school,

4 I looked all around.

5 Hey, here is my coat

6 in the Lost and Found!

1 Look-Alike Day

2 We are copycats

3 on Look-Alike Day.

4 We call our friends

5 and dress the same way.

1 Some Opposites at School

2 Time to work

3 and time to play.

4 Today, tomorrow, and yesterday.

5 Up and down.

6 Sun and clouds.

7 In and out.

138

8 Quiet and LOUD.

1 When I Shared My Cat

2 When I shared my cat,

3 he was scared about that.

4 He tried to eat

5 our parakeet.

6 He ran around fast.

7 But we got him at last!

1 The Estimation Jar

2 How many beans

3 in the estimation jar?

4 25?

5 50?

6 110?

7 No. Wait. Wait.

8 Let me guess again!

Who Am I?

2 You throw me.

3 You catch me.

4 You bounce me on the wall. (Ouch!)

5 You dribble.

6 You kick me.

7 I am a red rubber _____!

The Last Day of School

2 Good-bye, my school friends.

3 We really had a ball.

4 I will see you in the summer

5 or back at school

6 next fall.

1 At the Library

2 Every day

3 at the librar-y,

4 every book

5 you see

6 is free!

1 I Trade at the Bank

2 My piles of pennies

3 grow taller and taller.

4 I roll up 100

5 and trade for one dollar.

At the Ice Cream Store

1 At the Ice Cream Store

2 It is hard to pick

3 which one to lick

4 and which kind of cone

5 to munch and crunch.

The Police

1 The Police

2 I wave at the police car.

3 It is black and it is white.

4 The police keep me safe

5 all day and all night.

1 The Fire Fighters

2 Fire! Fire!

3 9-1-1

4 The firefighters stay

5 till the work is done.

1 What the Mailman Had

1 Some Animal Transportation

2 A letter for mom.

3 A letter for dad.

4 That is what the mailman had.

5 One more thing!

6 A box for me!

7 A birthday gift!

8 What could it be?

2 The little frog has legs to hop.

3 The monkey swings from tree to tree.

4 The green snake wiggles.

5 The birds all fly.

6 The penguin swims in the cold cold sea.

1 All Kinds of Transportation

2 A bus,

3 a train,

4 a boat,

5 a plane,

6 some trucks and cars

7 out on the street,

8 a taxicab,

9 and my two feet!

1 What Trucks Do

2 Trucks dig.

3 Trucks crunch.

4 Trucks munch recycling

5 for their lunch.

1 When You Ride a Bike

2 Stop at every

3 stop sign.

4 Show turns

5 with your hand.

6 Always wear

7 your helmet.

8 It can save you

9 when you land.

1 The Train

2 I show my ticket.

3 Then clackity-clack,

4 clackity-clack,

5   clackity-clack.

6   The train goes speeding

7   down the track.

1   What is Fast, Faster, Fastest?

2   My skateboard is fast.

3   My scooter is faster.

4   But when I am late,

5   my bike is just great!

The Plane Ride

2 My seat belt goes click.

3 Up, up we go.

4 Then out my window,

5 clouds put on a show!

Go to the Moon

2 Put on your helmet.

3 Put on your suit.

4 They will count down to zero.

5 Then off we will shoot!

6 10, 9, 8, 7, 6, 5, 4, 3, 2, 1, 0

7 Blastoff!

1 Our Flag

2 Our flag! Our flag!

3 You are red, white, and blue.

4 We stand and we say

5 the pledge to you.

1 We Recycle

2 We recycle each paper.

3 We recycle each can.

4 We help save the earth.

5 That is our plan!

1 All Over the World

2 All over the world, kids

1 In All Kinds of Weather

2 A warm rain.

3 run and jump,

4 play with friends,

5 hug their parents,

6 go to school.

7 Just like me!

8 That is cool!

3 A lot of snow.

4 A sunny sky.

5 A big rainbow.

6 In all kinds of weather,

7 we still play together.

1 The Fall Leaves

2 The wind blew. Yahoo!

3 The leaves are falling

1 The Apples in Fall

2 Yellow, red, or green.

3 Shiny, hard, and clean.

4 on my head,

5 brown,

6 yellow,

7 orange,

8 and red.

4 Sour or sweet.

5 Crunchy to eat!

1 Snow

2 Snowflakes

3 Snowfall

4 Snowman

5 Snowball

6 Snowball fight

7 one and all!

1 In My Mittens

2 I wiggle my pinkie.

3 I wiggle my thumb.

4 Then inside my mittens

5 my hands are not numb!

1 When It Snows

2 It is very quiet

3 when it snows.

4 The snowflakes softly

5 tap my nose.

1 The Spring Things

2 The days are warm.

3 The baby birds

4 flap flap

5 their baby wings.

6 The flowers grow.

7 The winds blow.

8 It must be spring!

1 In the Wind

2 In windy weather

3 grab your hat.

4 But let your kite

5 go way up high,

6 red and yellow

7 in the clear, blue sky.

1 In Summer

2 On a hot summer day,

3 we try to stay

4 as cool and wet

5 as we can get.

1 All Year Round

2 In fall we walk on yellow leaves.

3 In winter we walk on ice and snow.

4 In spring we walk on flower beds.

5 In summer we walk on grass and then,

6 in fall, we start all over again.

1 On Halloween

2 A black hat.

3 A small hat.

4 A funny hat.

5 A tall hat.

6 What will I be on Halloween?

7 A bat?

8 A pumpkin?

9 A clown?

10 A queen?

1 On Thanksgiving

2 Thank you for my family.

3 Thank you for my friends.

4 Thank you for the big blue sky.

5 Thanks for turkey and pumpkin pie.

1 For Dr. Martin Luther King, Jr.

2 For Dr. Martin Luther King,

3 freedom

4 peace

5 friends

6 and love

7 were all of the important things.

1 The 100th Day of School

2 We are counting the days

3 in lots of ways.

4 After 99,

5 comes the 100th day!

1. On Valentine's Day

2. I gave everyone

3. a red valentine.

4. Then I ate up

5. my candy

6. and read

7. all of

8. mine!

On St. Patrick's Day

1 It is hard to catch

2 a leprechaun.

3 You think you have him.

4 But then he is gone!

The Days of the Week

1 Count them up.

2 Seven days.

4 Five for school.

5 Two for play.

6 Monday

7 Tuesday

8 Wednesday

9 Thursday

10 Friday

11 Saturday

12 and Sunday.

1 The Colors

2 The sun is yellow.

3 Apples are red.

4 The sky and the sea are blue.

5 The grass is green.

6 Owls are brown.

7 The night is black. Whooo.

1 The Shapes

2 The playground has

3 rectangles,

4 circles,

5 and squares.

6 But there are no

7 triangles

8 Whooooo.

1 The Numbers

2 The numbers like to

3 stay in line.

4 1, 2, 3, 4, 5, 6, 7, 8, 9.

5 The numbers like to

6 do their tricks,

7 like 3 plus 3 always makes 6!

8 anywhere.

1 Some Bug Colors

2 What is green? a grasshopper

3 What is red? ants on a tree

4 What is orange? a butterfly

5 What is black? this spider on me!

1 The Spider in the Car

2 Hey, little spider

3 living in our car.

4 Your spider web tells me

5 where you are.

6 I wish you would decide

7 to go and live outside.

1 A Yucky Bug

2 I have seen an ant.

3 I have seen a bee.

4 I have seen a fly.

5 I have seen a flea.

6 But this little bug

7 is the yuckiest bug

8 that I will ever ever ever see.

1 Our Class Has Silkworms

2 Our silkworms get fat.

3 They eat lots of leaves.

4 Then they make the cocoons

5 that they know how to weave.

6 Inside they grow wings

7 that they show in the spring.

1 The Bees

2 Bees are fuzzy.

3 Bees are buzzy.

4 But stay far away.

5 Bees do not like to play.

A Star With Wings

1 A Star With Wings

2 Sometimes it seems

3 like a little star

4 has fallen

5 from the sky.

6 But when I see

7 the star has wings,

8 I know it is a firefly.

1 The Boy Ladybugs

2 Do the boy ladybugs

3 hear their name

4 and say *ugh?*

1 Some Animal Names

2 The woodpecker pecks.

3 The grasshopper hops.

4 The stingray stings.

178

5 I wish it would stop.

1 Some Baby Animals

2 A kitten is a baby cat.

3 A colt is a baby horse.

4 A calf can be a baby whale,

5 or a baby cow, of course.

1 A Lot of Eggs

2 Here is a blue egg.

3 Who is inside?

4 A baby robin.

5 What a surprise!

6 Here is a small egg.

7 Who is inside?

8 A baby fish.

9 What a surprise!

10 Here is a long egg.

180

11 Who is inside?

12 A baby snake.

13 What a surprise!

14 Here is an egg

15 in super-size.

16 A dinosaur!

17 What a surprise!

1 The Turtle

2 We helped out the turtle

3 who was crossing the street,

4 so he would not get squashed

5 by cars or by feet.

1 When Alligators Grow

2 Everybody seems to love

3 a baby alligator.

4 But when she is big and scary,

5 everybody seems to hate her.

1 The Great White Shark

2 The great white shark

3 does not go to sleep.

4 Does he ever get tired

5 of swimming in the deep?

1 If I Were an Octopus

2 I would call a friend.

3 I would drum a beat.

4 I would play a game.

5 I would eat a treat.

6 I would jump a rope.

7 I would watch TV.

8 All at the very same time, you see!

1 A Penguin

2 Slip, slide,

3 she glides on her tummy.

4 Jump, dive,

5 she eats something yummy.

1 Who Is It?

2 This mammal has

3 a whale of a tail.

4 Watch out!

5 It spouts water

6 all about!

1 I Sleep in a Cave

2 I go very deep

3 in a cave to sleep

4 until birds in spring

5 begin to cheep.

6 Who am I?

1 All About Bats

2 At night,

3 the bats all fly around.

4 In the day,

5 the bats sleep upside down!

1 Some Animal Homes

2 Crabs live in sand.

3 Snails live on leaves.

4 Birds live in trees.

5 Whales live in seas.

6 My cat is the home

7 for lots and lots of fleas.

The Silly Farm

2 The sheep said oink.

3 The duck said moo.

4 The farmer said cock-a-doodle-doo.

5 The cows just didn't know what to do.

In the Morning

1 In the Morning

2 Go milk the cow.

3 Look under the hens.

4 Then hold your nose!

5 Feed the pigs in their pens.

What the Sheep Wear

1 What the Sheep Wear

2 In winter, their wool

3 is warm and full.

4 In spring, they don't wear

5 anything.

1 The Pink Pigs

2 The fat, pink pigs

3 roll in the mud

4 because it is no fun

5 to get a piggy sunburn

6 in the hot, summer sun.

1 100

2 I would not like to have

3 100 brothers or

4 or 100 little sisters.

5 But I would like to have

6 100 dogs or

7 100 cats with whiskers.

1 What Can You Pop?

2 Pop a drink box.

3 Pop a sack.

4 Pop your bubble gum.

5 Yum! Yum! Yum!

6 Pop a trash bag.

7 Pop some popcorn

8 Pop the bubble wrap.

9 Snap! Snap! Snap!

Please Tickle Me

2 Tickle me one.

3 Tickle me two.

4 Tickle me under my sock and shoe.

5 Tickle me three.

6 Tickle me four.

7 Tickle until I scream, "No more!"

Some Somersault Fun

2 Come and join us.

3 Have some fun.

4 Do some somersaults in the sun.

5 We do somersaults

6 in the park.

7 We only stop when it gets dark.

1 It Fits

2 An egg fits well

3 inside its shell.

4 A banana must feel

5 snug in its peel.

6 And my skin hides

7 all my insides!

1 The Rain

2 Out on the farm

3 and all over town,

4 it never rains up.

5 It always rains down.

1 I Like to Be Silly

2 It starts with a smile

3 that shows on my face.

4 But soon I am laughing

5 all over the place.

1 How Do You Do, Glue?

2 How do you do, glue?

3 Take a look, book.

4 Never again, pen.

5 See you later, calculator!

Made in the USA